GET IT DONE

Hard-Hitting Motivation for Authors

JONATHAN YANEZ

Archimedes Books

ACKNOWLEDGMENTS

If you think this book is awesome at all it's only because I have a pack of rabid ARC Wolves, a wonderful editor and a talented cover artist. Thank you for your help.

ARC WOLVES

Kelly
Athena
Eagle Eyes
Lois

Editor - Kimberly
Cover Illustrator - Steve

CHAPTER ONE

What does this guy know about writing and why should I listen to him?

Here's the hard and fast version, or you can read further and get the whole story. I'm a six-figure author with thirty plus titles published. I've been both traditionally and independently published. Two of my series have been optioned for film and a third series is currently being adapted into a mobile video game.

I've launched my own merchandise line with items inspired by my series. I'm a *USA Today* and international bestseller. I'm president of my chapter's California Writer's Club. I've won the Jack London Award for my contributions to literature. I'm also a founding member of The Archers Rest Society (I just like to call it "The Society" because it sounds more cryptic, but my wife made me change this part so you would know the actual name). As part of The Archers Rest

Society, we put together events for high-level authors to network with industry professionals.

I usually don't talk about my journey, where I've come from or what I've done. Most of this comes from not liking to talk about myself and the other part comes from me not caring what I've accomplished in the past, but rather what I'm accomplishing now.

I started off in sales, and I didn't know it then, but all the "no's" I was taking on a daily basis were thickening my skin for my career as an author. I knew I always liked stories and wanted to write, but I needed this thing called money to support myself, and as you well know, it's difficult for beginning writers to make a decent income.

Over the five years I spent in sales and management, I would write off and on when things got rough. It was an outlet for me. I was never fully happy in that job; it was a necessary evil. I needed money and the raises and title changes over that five-year course were just enough to keep me in check.

Eventually, I had a life-altering decision to make. I hit rock bottom at my job. I was working sixty plus hours a week, six days a week, with the next promotion dangling in front of me.

I had to ask myself a tough question. Is this where I wanted to be for the rest of my life? I was at the point where I didn't even want my boss's title anymore. I saw how many hours he was putting in for our company and how stressed he was. I decided that wasn't for me.

I knew this was a crossroads in my life. On one hand, I could stay and build someone else's vision, or I could take the leap and build my own. I use the word "vision" instead of "dream" here because I think we tend to be overly dramatic when we say we're following our dreams. It sounds easy and poetic, when in truth, it's a hard road to be walked, full of hours of work. I call it "creating our vision."

After I made the decision to work for myself and create my own vision, I really put my back against the wall. I quit my job with no other plan but to write and cashed out my 401K.

I wrote my first book called *The Beast Within* and started to query while I worked on the next. As you can imagine, and many of you know, the query process doesn't exactly move at the speed of light. That 401K money was being eaten up quickly.

Since I was fifteen years old, working out and exercise have always been a passion of mine. I've exercised on a pretty consistent basis since then. I was looking for a part time job to keep myself afloat while I worked on my books, so I started personal training at my gym.

Well, long story longer, I was picked up by a traditional publishing house. I spent almost five years with them before I realized I could make more money independently publishing. It was two years ago that I made the change. I now write fulltime, making more than my boss's boss at my previous job.

I have nothing against traditional publishing and still have a great relationship with my publisher. There are pros and cons to each path. You have to make the right decision on what you want from writing and the best way to get there. For me, I want to own my own company, work for myself, and make enough money to support my family. I'm able to do this by being an independent writer.

Enough about me now. I want to share with you a few of

the tricks and truths I've picked up along the way. Between my sales background and personal training tenure, I think it might just be the kick in the pants you need to take your own author career to the next level.

CHAPTER TWO

Bear Your Burden Well

"Don't pray for an easier life, pray for strength to bear the one you have well." – Bruce Lee

We're all different people, we all come from very different backgrounds, and thus we struggle with very different things in this world. As writers, this also holds true. We're English majors, creative writing majors, we're mothers and fathers, twenty somethings, and retirees.

We've all had different experiences in this life that have for better or worse shaped who we are today. We hit the keyboard with different outlooks on the world and different obstacles calling for us that try and suck our writing time up like a black hole.

Compared to writing, cleaning the house, doing the dishes, and folding the laundry seem like strolls along the beach. The point is that writing is hard. Writing is beyond hard; it's an act of pure will that gets us behind that keyboard. Whatever the distraction might be for you or the reason why you just can't write, know you're not alone.

The number one thing that tries to pry my fingers off the keyboard is the marketing side of our business. There always seems to be a newsletter that needs to be prepared or an email that must be answered. Don't even get me started on social media; that thing is a nightmare for authors' word counts.

The good news is that training yourself to bear your burden and getting your butt in the chair to write gets easier. Like anything in life, the more and more you practice, the better and better you'll get. So too, the easier and easier hitting your word counts will become.

Writing and the routine of writing will become less of a struggle, I promise. One day you'll look back and wonder how you met your word count so quickly. It'll be the same amount of words you used to struggle to get down before and then you'll realize the words are still the same words. The words themselves haven't gotten easier on their own all of a sudden. It's you who has gotten stronger.

Get it done, day in and day out, whatever your writing schedule looks like for you, hold yourself to it like someone clutching to a life raft in a hurricane.

Early in my career, hitting two thousand new words each day was my goal. I'd try to get it done in a few writing sessions throughout the day. When I learned the writing technique I'm about to share with you in the next chapter, I realized how I could double my word count to four thousand words a day and in half the time.

CHAPTER THREE

One Word at a Time

*"The Journey of a thousand miles begins with a single step." –
Lao Tzu*

I'm sure you've all heard this quote before. It holds true for
authors more than anyone. With each word we place on the
screen or write down on paper, we are a step closer to
finishing whatever book we are working on.

One word, one sentence, one paragraph, one page, one
chapter at a time; it all adds up. Progress is progress, my
friends, and that means a hundreds words, a page, a chapter is
something to be proud of accomplishing.

We all have different capacities for work. What might
seem like nothing to you is astronomical to others. What
might seem like a monster word count to you may be a cake-

walk for another author. The idea isn't to compare yourself to anyone else but yourself. If you're making strides every day to be a better author than the person you see in the mirror in the mornings, you're doing something right.

I have a personal writing goal of four thousand words a day, six days a week. That ensures that I'm able to release a book a month on schedule with built-in time in case things go awry at the editor's (this has never happened, by the way; she's awesome and in fact usually saves my deadline) or beta readers take longer than usual to get back to me or any number of things that go on in an author's worst nightmare.

To some people, four thousand words a day sounds like the ravings of a madman, a lunatic so hyped up on caffeine that he doesn't shower every day and his neighbors hate him because his front lawn hasn't been mowed in weeks, but enough about me. The point is there are other authors I know personally who write well over four thousand words a day. I know authors who are hitting word counts in the sum of ten thousand words plus each day.

Trust me, if I were to try and do that, my brain would be oatmeal and not the good kind with brown sugar or cinnamon; just plain old oatmeal. I've tried hitting those ten thousand word days, and through pure determination, I've made it happen, but for me, that's not a sustainable, long-term goal.

What I mean by that is that I'm not able to put more than one or two ten-thousand-word days in a row before I feel like a dementor has come down and sucked the very life out of me. I'm an animal built to grind, but I'm built for the long haul not crazy word counts in ten-thousand-word sprints.

I know that about myself and I'm okay with it. Now I know I could put a day or two of work like that in if I absolutely had to. If Stephen King called and asked if I could have a book for him in a week, that he had film rights ready to go and our names would appear side by side on the cover, you best believe I'm taking my tent to Starbucks and I'm riding the crazy train to get that book done. However, for the day in and day out grind, four thousand words is my comfortable goal.

Enter the Flow State

"What is this magical flow state you speak of?"

Well, I'm glad you asked.

Athletes have understood this term for years and it applies to authors as well. The flow state is a degree of focus you reach when you are fully engaged in an activity such as writing.

Ever have those writing sprints or sessions where you are one hundred percent engaged and the scenes are flowing to you like the wine in Valhalla? Maybe you knew it or maybe you didn't, but you entered a flow state where you were engrossed with your work with zero distractions.

To enter this state, set up writing sprints for yourself. What works for me is four thirty-minute sprints throughout the day. In a thirty-minute undistracted run, I know I can get one thousand new words on the page.

I turn off all distractions, including my phone, Facebook, Instagram, and all the other things that seek to steal my time. For those thirty minutes, I just go. There's no going back and editing either. Stopping your rhythm and going back to change a sentence you just wrote takes you out of the flow state. Give yourself permission to misspell words and write sentences that might not be your very best and get the words on the page.

Trust me, there will be plenty of editing phases for you to go back and fix all of this. For many, the first draft is the most difficult. On this first draft, just worry about getting words on the page and that's it.

But I don't have time

You'll find time for things that are most important to you. Right now, I stay at home with my two-year-old daughter. Besides writing, I hit the gym six times a week and model part time.

The gym keeps me sane and healthy. Modeling is something I've been phasing out due to it coming in last on my list of priorities. I usually do four to five shoots a year. It's fun, great money, and it gets me out of the house. I've been able to do shoots for companies like Nissan, Bank of America, and PlayStation.

All this to say my schedule is bananas. Despite this, my career as an author is important to me, so I find the time to write.

I stay at home with my little warrior empress. That means carving out times of the day to get a sprint in and do everything else book-related. Writing is the most important thing, so most days, my schedule looks like this. I've taught myself to wake up early and get a sprint in as well as take care of any emails or messages in the early morning before she's up.

Between seven and eight, I hear little bare feet padding on the hardwood floor. She bursts into my office with a Cheshire grin on her face, swiping at her auburn hair with chubby forearms, trying to get it out of her face. She runs to me with all the power of an NFL linebacker and hurls herself at me, all the time saying, "Daddy! Daddy!" like I'm the most important person on the planet.

That's my cue to close my laptop no matter what I may be in the middle of. It's on me, no one else, if I didn't get my first or second writing sprint (one to two thousand words) in. No excuses. If I didn't get it done, then I have to make that up somewhere during the rest of my day.

My next window of opportunity comes right after lunch, when the heiress goes down for her nap. Usually, this is from noon to two, but anyone who has kids will tell you that there are always exceptions to the rule. In those two hours that she's normally down for a nap, I can get two more writing sprints in, including more answering emails, social media, and the hundred other things we have to do as owners of our own business.

The last window of opportunity comes at night when my girls are asleep. Not every night, but normally, I can get another window of work in between nine and ten pm. This is my last chance to hit my four-thousand-word count for the day. Usually, I only have to write the last one thousand words, but if I missed one or two of the sprints earlier that day, it's on me to get it down now.

Of course, there are exceptions to these rules. Weekends are a lot easier to work. Sometimes family comes and visits and I can get more done. On the flip side of that coin, I may be up against a deadline and need to wake up a few hours earlier or stay up a few hours later. Or if we're really cooking with fire, both.

This is what it looks like broken down. This is normally how it works, but there are always days where my best laid plans falter: my daughter wakes up early, she doesn't take her usual nap, or I have a meeting during the day. I share it with you to give you ideas of where you can find writing sprints throughout the day.

6AM 1 – 2 writing sprints and answering emails

8AM Josephine is up and it's time to color My Little Ponies

12PM Jo naps, 1 – 2 writing sprints and social media

2PM Jo is up and ready to go outside and play with our dogs AKA wolves

445PM My wife is home and we have family time.

6PM Gym

7PM Dinner, shower, family time, last chance to get in any missed writing

10PM Sleep

I don't want you to think any of this is easy. In fact, I care about your career so much, I'm going to be brutally honest with you. Being a full time author is hard. It's going to push you and grow you in ways you never thought possible. You'll be exhausted, have to sacrifice time with friends, and television will be nonexistent in your life. But I promise you it's worth it.

There is nothing like being able to work from your own home, inspire readers around the world, and build something that will last for years to come.

If you don't have time then find it, sleep less, sacrifice television. I don't allow myself to make excuses and I care about you too much to let you do the same. Do it with passion or not at all.

Now this is all true if you are serious about making a living as an author. If this is just a side gig for you or you don't care about building a business, of course you can just write whenever the spirit compels you to. However, if you want to work for yourself and make a great living as a writer, then it is possible, and this is how you do it.

CHAPTER FOUR

Get Back Up

*"Strength and growth come through continuous effort and struggle." –
Napoleon Hill*

We all fall down. We all have bad days. We're all going to be let down, disappointed, angry, and frustrated. That's fine; these are all human emotions. If you can master your emotions, you'll be a force to be reckoned with.

Not every book is going to be a best seller. Not every book is going to make your career, get a movie deal, or bring in five digits. I promise if you keep writing, those opportunities will come.

After thirty plus books written, only two have been optioned for film. As much as I would like all of them to have been best sellers and made into Hollywood movies and net me a million dollars plus, that's just not the case.

I have some good news for you, though, my friends. If you keep on writing, growing, and producing work, you'll grab Opportunity's attention sooner or later. It won't be able to ignore you. It took me five years and twenty-something books for me to finally break through. I hope you can do it in less, but even if you can't, it will come.

Think about it this way. When you put your back against the wall and take away all the excuses, you'll have one of two options. Either you will quit or you will succeed. It's as simple as that. Either you'll fight and keep on fighting until you win or you'll give up.

The great thing about writing is that you really can't be defeated by anyone or anything else. You can only give up. You can only defeat yourself.

My very first book was called *The Beast Within*. I queried one hundred agents and publishing houses before I got a single yes. I didn't point my finger or blame other people when those rejections came. I looked at myself first to see if there was anything I could be doing better.

My strategy was to send queries out in batches of ten or twenty at a time and wait to hear back before doing the same thing until I reached one hundred. If I reached one hundred without a yes, then I would write another book and do the same thing and another and another after that until something happened. I refused to break.

Knowing what I know now, I would have just independently published those books, but that was part of my own growing experience and a chapter in my own story.

I still personal train part time, not because I have to, but because I enjoy it. I tell all my clients at the gym and the writers I consult that you're allowed to have bad days, get angry and frustrated, but you're not allowed to give up.

One thing that has really helped with dealing with rejection is giving myself a pre-set window to be angry. When I started practicing this technique, I would give myself a day. I would let myself dwell on why it didn't work out or feel sorry for myself and be frustrated.

Over time, I realized that a full day was way too long. I didn't like spending that much time dwelling on something I couldn't control. I had things to do. What's done is done. I just wanted to move on. Nowadays, I think there is almost something wrong with me. I'm way too optimistic. I've been said no to, ignored, and rejected so many times now, I've lost track.

Even being shut down or cast to the side so many times, I've still been able to come out on top in my career. Now when doors are shut or opportunities are withheld from me for whatever reason, I shrug and move on to working on my next project. Literally, I spend seconds on a failed opportunity, understanding there is nothing I can do, and choose to spend my energy on something I can control, usually my next book.

Over the years, I've built up such an immunity to rejection I almost embrace it because I know it will make me stronger. Every time a door is shut, I try to learn something. I take it as an opportunity to grow.

There was an instance just a few weeks ago when I received nothing but yesses on various projects, all the doors were opened, and it seemed way too easy. I thought to myself, "Self, maybe you're setting the bar too low. Maybe you need to shoot higher if all these people are saying yes to you now."

That same night, I contacted a few high-level executives at some companies you'd know to see if they would be interested in a few projects I had to pitch. Think the very highest you can shoot for and you're close. I either got rejected by them or ignored altogether but as weird as this is, I kind of liked it. I knew I was putting myself out there again and I will continue to do so until the day I die.

There are great things waiting for you on the opposite side of fear. For those of you willing to take the leap and put your back against the wall, to look your fear in the face and roar into the night, you'll find opportunities.

Work, struggle, fall, and get back up, and learn why you fell. Then do it again and again and again until the falls don't hurt so much, until falling and getting back up become so second nature to you it doesn't even feel like you've fallen at all.

No such thing as writer's block

I know this is an unpopular viewpoint to hold. As writers, we want an easy way out and it's an excuse I've seen other writers make from day one. I've been writing fulltime for the last seven years, and if I had a gold coin for every time I've heard this excuse, I'd put Smaug's Horde to shame.

And I can already hear it now. "But I know writer's block is real because sometimes when I sit down, I just don't know what to write." Or "Writer's block is an actual thing. I've heard it from so many different authors."

If writer's block is a real thing, then why doesn't it exist in any other profession? I've never heard of plumber's block or teacher's block. A rebuttal I've heard to this is that writer's block exists because we're creating and as such sometimes the "muse" or "inspiration" doesn't come to us while we're at work.

To this I say, whose fault is that? At some point, you have to take charge of your own business as a writer. If your magical muse isn't speaking while you sit in front of the keyboard, then maybe you needed to outline. If you don't know where the story is headed next, then maybe you should have been better prepared once you sat down at the keyboard.

I'm a pantser, and no, that doesn't mean I run around jerking down people's pants. The term "pantser" in the writing community means that I write by the seat of my pants. I don't outline. I usually have an idea where the story is going to end, but that's about it. Half the fun for me when it comes to writing is joining my characters in the adventure and discovering what's going on along with them.

Because I don't outline, I am constantly thinking of what is going to happen next in my story. I look for inspiration everywhere in my life to feed this hungry beast. I find ideas while hanging out with my wife and daughter, listening to music, watching television, on the rare occasion this happens, and of course, reading or listening to other books.

A funny thing is that the mortgage comes at the same time every month. You best believe that muse is showing up on time when I sit down to write.

Now this is not to say that sometimes writing is not harder than others. I get that; trust me, I do. I'm not somehow magically immune to having rough days of writing. There will be times I just can't focus. But guess what, I don't write that off as writer's block. I take responsibility for my career as an author and I still hit my word count.

This may mean that I have to go grab some coffee, turn off or on my epic music soundtrack; heck, I might even have to go to the gym to get my head right, but I do it and reset and get back to work. I don't believe in writer's block, but I know excuses are a real thing. I refuse to let myself make them.

I'm not where I am today because I let myself off the hook. Over the years, I've taught myself discipline and you can too.

CHAPTER FIVE

Share and Don't Live in Fear

Everything you want is on the other side of fear – Jack Canfield

You are capable of incredible things. You were meant to write the book only you can write. No one sounds exactly like you, no one cares about your story like you. As you find success and meet other struggling authors, don't be afraid to help them.

No one runs this path to author success alone. If you think you've done this all by your lonesome, you're lying to yourself. I hate to break the news to you, brothers and sisters, but everyone from Margaret Atwood to George Lucas had help. No one did this by themselves.

Now this help doesn't mean they were taken under some big wig's wing and privately mentored, although it can. You can receive help and knowledge by reading articles, listening to podcasts, or speaking to those who have done it. If you want to argue this point name me one person who reached the top of their author success completely on their own. Go ahead, I'll wait.

Everyone has help in one form or another. I am no different and neither are you. And that's okay. We all need to learn from others who have done this before us, learn from those who are innovating the process now, and reach back to help those behind us.

Now I'm not saying you need to blast out to the ether every time you reach a milestone and give exact detail on how you did it. I mean, you can if you want to. Don't let me rain on your parade. You do you.

What I am saying is that when others reach out for help, take a few minutes to answer their question. I'm not claiming to be busier than any of you, but I am pretty freaking busy. Between writing a book a month, staying at home with my daughter, spending time with my wife, working out six times a week, and modeling, I hardly have any time to myself. Still, when I receive those emails and Facebook messages asking questions, I always make time to answer.

These answers may just be pointing people in the right direction or may take a day or two for me to respond back, but I do what I can to give back. One thing I've learned in this jungle we call authorship is not to be too accessible.

"What do you mean by that?" you ask. "I thought you just said to help others and don't be a jerk."

I did.

I always respond back to questions or inquiries, but a trick I've learned is not to feel pressured to have to respond back right away. Waking up to ten emails asking me questions, six Facebook messages, fourteen Instagram comments, and forty Facebook comments can be overwhelming. Add this to my normal day of one to two hours at the gym and four thousand words and it's downright anxiety mode.

I just take a deep breath, remind myself that I will get to all the emails and messages, but I don't have to do it right then at that exact moment, and I go about my routine. My family and business have to take priority, but once I have a few things off my plate for the day, then I give myself the okay to go in and answer a few comments and questions.

You need to take care of yourself first before you can pull those up beside you. That's the main reason I haven't written a nonfiction book up until this point. I wanted to get my own house/business in order before I felt comfortable going out and encouraging others to do the same.

I didn't want to hand out information as a brand new author or someone who hasn't reached a certain level of success. I want to be the leader who leads from the front and tell you because I've been in the trenches with you. I'm still in the trenches with you today. I'm still learning and getting stronger, but I've been there and I can help you by practicing what I preach.

When I see other authors offering classes and courses writing books on how to be successful and I look at their sales, it leaves a strange taste in my mouth. How are you going to learn from someone who hasn't done it themselves?

If you haven't already noticed, a lot of my analogies are going to be about health and fitness because that's also close to my heart. I used to work at a gym that will remain nameless, but it has a 24 in its name.

I worked there with a group of other personal trainers and

we had this one personal trainer who was overweight. Now I never make fun of overweight people because I love them, especially those motivated to do something to make a healthier change. There's nothing but love and respect in my heart for anyone trying to better themselves.

With that said, there are also questions that come to mind when there is an overweight personal trainer giving instruction to clients on how they should lose weight and exercise. I knew this personal trainer and there was nothing medically wrong with him besides the fact that he was lazy.

I told myself then I would never be that person. I would always lead by example and never ask anything of my clients or those I mentor to do something I wasn't willing to do myself. I lead from the front; always have and always will.

So help those around you. Don't be afraid to share information as if by giving someone else who is asking for help information or resources or a lead or a connection that it will somehow cut into your own success.

That's playing a scared game and you're better than that. Sharing information and helping others doesn't make you weaker; it makes you stronger and it builds important relationships around you.

The very worst case scenario is that by sharing a contact or information, that contact or piece of information is discovered by the masses and you help a ton of people, but since so many people are using it, perhaps it isn't as effective as it once was. Guess what? You'll adapt to survive and you'll find another contact or resource that is just as good or better.

I'm just going to get really specific here. For authors, these resources or information can be a killer cover artist, a great editor, or maybe a hot new genre that's selling.

Now I'm not going to go out and shout any of this from a mountain top. I'm not trying to force this information down anyone's throat. Frankly, I'm too busy for any of that. But if another traveler comes asking me for water, and I have water to give, you bet I'm sharing.

And if word gets out and my contact or resource is no longer effective, I will find a way to move forward because we are survivors and we don't know the meaning of surrender.

Surround Yourself with a Strong Pack

Anyone who knows me well knows I love wolves. From the tattoo on my shoulder to my husky and Alaskan malamute, I love everything there is about these animals.

One of the many reasons I love them is because they are strong on their own but better in a pack. These predators are fierce but deadly when they stand together.

I've modeled my own career after a wolf pack to the extent my newsletter for my fiction books is called the Pack. Along your author journey, think of these animals.

We already talked about how no one makes it down this road alone. It is imperative that you find your pack and you share information and learn and grow from one another as you do.

Iron sharpens iron. Two heads are better than one. I can go on and on with sayings, but I'll just give you a personal example. I've partnered with a few authors who are either at my same level or ahead of me and taken my business to the next level through these relationships.

"But, wolf guy, author man," you ask. "How do I find authors like this?"

That answer is simple. Put yourself out there and start talking with other authors. There is no shortage of Facebook groups, author forums, or Reddit posts out there for authors. Befriend them, comment on their posts, and post on these platforms. Maybe read one of their books so you can talk with them about something they can relate to. The most important thing here is to be part of the conversation, even if you're not leading the conversation. Sometimes it's enough just to have a horse in the race.

In my experience, nine out of ten authors you try and connect with would love to talk with you. Of course there is always that one out of ten that will ignore you or tell you that they're not interested, and guess what, that's okay.

Not everyone has to like you or want to be your friend. I think I'm the bee's knees and I want to be friends with nearly everyone. Well, not everyone feels the same. Guess what? It's story time.

When I began this writing journey, I reverted back to my sales days and started talking to and befriending as many authors as I could. This is especially beneficial when you are looking for newsletter swaps, but we won't get into those. That's a whole other book on how to launch your novel after it's written.

Anywho, I was adding authors on Facebook and sending messages and just trying to get to know my fellow writers. I heard once that the fastest way to learn a foreign language is to immerse yourself in the culture. Well, I took that to heart here and threw myself head first into meeting and connecting with like-minded writers.

As you can probably guess, not everyone was super friendly. I had a few completely ignore me. I had a few tell me they weren't interested in helping other authors, and guess what? It was totally fine, life went on, the sun set in the west and rose in the east the next day.

I held on to those who were willing to befriend me. We share information about the industry, making both of our businesses better. I've co-written with a handful of them and even hang out with a lot of them in real life now. I talk to these guys on the phone and I know we have each other's back no matter what.

Funny thing about some of those friend requests I sent out that never got answered as well as the no's I received. When my own books really took off and I made top seller lists, was asked on podcasts and to speak at events, guess who came around? Yep, not all of them, but friends requests I had sent months ago were suddenly accepted. Weird how that happens, huh?

After a few years, you'll get a kind of spidey sense about these things. You'll be able to tell who your pack is and see the same drive in others that lives inside of you. I have a saying that sums this up. It's the highest praise I can give anyone. "The animal in me recognizes the animal in you." To me, that means the same drive and determination that resides in the core of my being, that same thing, I see in you.

I've been able to run with a group of authors who are six- and seven-figure writers. They're industry professionals and see the future and where it is taking us. These guys aren't afraid to share information with one another. They see the value in collaboration.

Find your pack. Trust me, they are out there looking for you too. When you find your brothers and sisters, keep them close. Lift one another up. Reach back, offer aid to those behind you.

CHAPTER SIX

Haters Gonna Hate

Players gonna play, haters gonna hate, shake it off. – Taylor Swift

I once heard a story of a YouTube video of a chubby little baby girl playing with her even chubbier puppy friend. The little girl was squealing and laughing while the puppy's tail was wagging a hundred miles an hour and he was bouncing around giving her licks of affection.

This video went on to be an internet sensation with millions of likes and even more views. Out of the millions of souls this little girl and her puppy brought happiness to, there were three thumbs-down on the video. Three people out of millions for some reason found fault with this tiny owner and her pup.

This is a perfect example of how you will never please

everyone. If this little angel with her plump puppy aren't going to do it, I have sad news for you, my friend, neither are we.

From JK Rowling to Walt Disney, everyone has his or her haters. It's just a fact of life. There are people out there who maybe just had a bad day and they take it out on your work. Maybe they're jealous, so they try and cut you down with their words. Maybe they're just an internet troll and this is their hobby on days that end with Y. Don't let them get to you; you're better than that.

This has been true for every book I have ever written. I always get one-star reviews. It's part of life. The faster you learn to embrace this, the better off you will be. Eventually, you'll get to the point where you read your one-star reviews to see if there is any validity to their claim.

I read all of my reviews because I know I'm not going to let words affect me. Through years of sales and rejection, I have callouses over my feelings two feet thick. There are two people on God's green Earth who I've given the power to affect me emotionally. One is my wife and the other is my daughter.

I refuse to give strangers the power over me to the point where their words have any sway over my emotions. I read my reviews now to find out if there are multiple one-star reviews that say the same thing. If that is the case, then maybe there is a learning opportunity for me or a chance to grow.

I don't recommend you start reading your lower-rated reviews until you know you can handle this process. If you're sensitive and you know that, don't put yourself through that torment.

I would encourage you to start working on your sensitivity when it comes to your work if you know that you don't take criticism well. Start off by reading a four- or three-star review. Understand that these people don't know you. One thing to also keep in mind is that people are brave behind the keyboard. They are willing to say things to you they would never say to your face.

Practice controlling your emotions. Once you've read a review and there are harsh words inside, it's up to you to be mentally strong enough not to let those words fester. Move on. Control what you can control. You can't control what reviews say, but you can control how much effort you're putting into your current work in process.

Throw yourself into your next project if words from others are bothering you. I'm not saying it's easy when you start, but it does get better. If you can set yourself up for successes here, then you'll be able to read all of your reviews one day and they won't bother you at all. Instead, you can use them to grow and get stronger and stronger until you are a force this world has never seen before. Okay, maybe not that crazy, but you get what point I'm trying to make here. My fiction side is starting to come out in my nonfiction writing.

Learn When to Say No

The main thing is to keep the main thing the main thing. I know that may not make sense at first, but trust me, it does. Say it a few times slowly and it works; it's not a typo. What it means is that if you want to write your book and you want to write books for a living, the main thing for you to do, your main job, is to guess what, that's right, write books.

Things will come to try and steal your time away. Some of these things will be an easy decision for you to say no to.

Staying up late and watching a show instead of going to sleep to wake up and write early is an easy no. So too is deciding to sleep in instead of waking up and getting to work.

Other things will attack you like a wolf in sheep's clothing. Opportunities will come that seem like a great way to spend your time, but in reality, they are stealing away precious hours for you to get your book written. Things like social media, creating book trailers, creating writing playlists, and on and on are not bad things in and of themselves. However, if they are cutting into your writing time, you need to say no.

You need to be greedy with your writing time. Protect it like Gollum protected the one ring. Okay, maybe not the best of analogies, but the point is that you say no to other things if it means getting between you and your word count.

While we're on the topic of protecting your writing time, start finding the best writing time in the day that works for you. Some people work better in the morning, some at night. I would encourage you to find the best time for you to write and stick to that but then branch out. Over the many years of writing, I've taught myself to be able to write at any time during the day.

I never want to use the time of day as an excuse not to write. Any excuse or anything I could use as a crutch not to put words on the screen I've eviscerated. I've taught myself to write with or without music, with or without caffeine, and not wait for the perfect time of the day to put my fingers on the keyboard.

This all goes back to learning how to say no to opportunities and protecting your writing time. I've had to say no to multiple photo shoots, co-writing opportunities, and more because I knew they would cut into my word count. The most important thing you can do as a writer is write that next book. Don't let anyone take that away from you.

CHAPTER SEVEN

No Timeframe on Success

*"Winners are not those who never fail but those who never quit." –
Edwin Louise Cole*

It's story time. Grab your favorite drink and listen up. During
World War II, a small group of survivors from a prison camp
was asked how they managed to hold on to hope and endure
when so many other prisoners did not.

One of the survivors shared some wisdom I've held close
to my heart. I think it applies to us as writers.

He told the person interviewing him that nearly all the
prisoners of war had some kind of hope. Many of them would
comfort themselves and each other, saying that if they just
held out to a specific date, then they would be saved. They
would use Christmas or Easter as dates in mind. They would
hinge their hope in being with their family and loved ones by

certain dates. These dates came and went. When they were not rescued, their spirit was crushed and they lost all hope or will to endure.

The survivor that was interviewed shared that he never lost hope, but neither did he put hope in a specific window of time. He just knew that he would be saved like he knew the sun would rise and set every day. He held on to the hope that it would happen but did not put a time constraint on the act.

I've spoken with so many writers who handicap themselves by doing this in their own careers. They tell themselves that by the first year or two years or three years of writing and publishing, they'll have reached their financial goal.

I've heard the same thing about the number of books they've written. I've heard authors tell me with a straight face that their first book will be a best seller all the way to book twenty will be the one they will be able to retire on.

Dear friends, do not do this to yourself. I'm not saying that having goals is a bad thing. Contrary to that, setting goals for yourself is a wonderful thing I do every day. I am saying that if you want this life as an author more than anything else, you will attain it. It won't matter if it takes you one year or five, five books or twenty-five. If you really want this and you are committed to working on it day in and day out, it will happen.

Know that success will find you, but it must find you at work. It found me after five years of writing full time and over a dozen books published. You are the master of your own ship and only you can write your origin story. Have goals but don't hinge your success on unrealistic expectations.

Remember there are only two options. Either you will write, learn, grow, and find success no matter how long it may or may not take or you will give up and choose to defeat yourself because you don't want to put in the work.

I know that may seem harsh, but I'm not here to be nice and tell you what you want to hear. I care about you too much to do that. I'm here to tell you the truth and do everything I can to get you to that next level.

When my clients at the gym tell me that our workouts are hard, my answer is, "If they're easy, we're doing something wrong."

Don't Save Your Ideas

Eighty-one percent of people want to write a book. Ninety-seven percent of those try to write a book and fail. I know we aren't math people here but stick with me. The fact that you are even trying to write a book sets you apart. The notion that you are reading this book right now further divides you from the herd.

You are taking the right steps and investing in your career. There's no better time to start than today, no better moment than now. Your mentality will have to change from "I want to write a book" to "I will write a book."

My man Yoda has a saying. "There is no try; only do or do not." Trying is all well and good. We all need to try our best at whatever we choose to tackle in life. But ultimately, we will get it done or we will not. Remember, no excuses; do or don't.

What are you waiting for? Do you need someone to take you by the hand and show you the way? Well, I'm here. Are you waiting for that perfect moment when inspiration will find you? Inspiration will find you at work. Are you waiting for a specific day and time? Today is the day and the time is now.

You are a force; don't let anyone ever tell you different.

You are a warrior of the written word and you can and you will get your book written. Whether this is your first attempt or your tenth.

I love wolves and huskies. I use the analogy of a pack of huskies pulling a sled in Alaska with my clients all the time. You were a husky pulling and straining at that sled alone. Now you and I are two huskies pulling at the sled together. When you start to surround yourself with like-minded, driven authors, you'll form your own pack, and as one, you'll move forward.

An important note to mention here is a pitfall I hear all the time. It's when an author starts their book, gets ten or twenty thousand words in, and stops. The dialogue with them goes something like this.

"Oh, but I have this great other idea I really want to write now. I'm going to put my current work in progress on hold to start this new idea."

"No you aren't."

"What?"

"You heard me," I say. "You have more inspiration and other ideas? That's wonderful; your imagination is firing on all cylinders. I love that about you. Now use those ideas you're coming up with in your current work in progress."

"Oh, I see what you mean, Jonathan," they say. "But I can't. I'm writing a science fiction story and my idea is about a dragon shifter." Or "My mystery novel just really wouldn't work with this new romance idea I have planned."

This is where I stare at them and just blink a few times.

Instead of shelving the book idea you were once in love with for that new shiny concept, use whatever idea you have in mind in your current work. If you're writing sci-fi, use a dragon race, or heck, use dragons in space. Readers of that genre love that kind of stuff. I've done it and I know many other authors doing it and we are making great money because we are writing what we want to read.

You have a mystery in the works, but you want to pump the brakes to start a romance novel? Why don't you put that romantic element into your mystery novel? I call that a win-win. Maybe there's some kind of black widow situation going on there.

Don't save your great ideas for future books. If you're excited about something, use it now. Tomorrow waits for no one. If you have a burning story inside of you, add it to your current work in progress. The best books are ones that have multiple angles and storylines interwoven through the overarching novel.

Don't be afraid to step out and write the stuff that you want to write. Have fun; that's the only way this is going to work long term. If you don't love writing and write what you love, we're in trouble.

Stay focused on your novel. Know that you will get it done. I'm rooting for you.

CHAPTER EIGHT

Stop Talking About it and Do it

*Start where you are. Use what you have. Do what you can –
Arthur Ashe*

I first came across this in school. I can't tell you how many
times I would hear my classmates talking about what they
were going to do, the things they were going to accomplish,
and the ideas they wanted to implement.

Now this is the part where I throw out a disclaimer. None
of that is bad in and of itself. I talk with my colleagues about
ideas and goals. There's nothing wrong with that. There is
something wrong with talking and only ever talking about it
with no action set in place. Words are dead without action to
back them up.

If I told you you're my friend then ignore all the emails
you send, messages you leave, and texts you write, what does

that tell you? It probably means I think you're more of a stalker and not my friend. It would take action on my part responding back, engaging you in conversation, and building bonds to move from just words to actual truth behind those words.

Writing is the same thing. I know so many authors who talk and talk and talk about writing their current book or their next book. Then I see pictures of them on Facebook on vacations, lounging around binging the next Netflix show, or complaining about how they have nothing to do and life is boring.

Still, they manage to complain how they don't have time to write their book. After a while, I get tired of hearing it and I'm surprised they don't. I'm a doer and I know you will be too.

Yes, talk and plan, but that talking and planning stage has to be the tip of the iceberg compared to what lies underneath the water. You know what lies underneath the water, don't you? Ninety percent of an iceberg is under water. When we take that analogy and apply it to writing versus talking, then the ten percent that lives above the waterline has to be the talking part and the other ninety percent below the water's surface has to be the actual doing.

Another benefit of not talking about doing something and actually doing it is people take you seriously. One of the many codes I live by outside of the obvious ones like "if you smelt it, you dealt it" is "Show me don't tell me."

Remember in *Jerry McGuire*, that famous line "Show me the money!" Yeah, it's just like that. Stop telling me that you have this great idea or that you are going to write your first book or your next book and go and do it.

This applies to first-time authors planning on penning their next book and authors who already have a book or ten out. I get it, writing a book, even your tenth book, can be daunting. I'm at thirty-something. I don't know the exact number because I don't care about going back and counting all of them from my traditional publisher, the short stories, the anthologies, the box sets, the so on and so on. Also, this goes back to the whole conversation where I don't like talking about myself or what I have done. I'm worried about what I'm doing now. If I wrote one hundred books, but the book I'm working on now tanks, then who cares what I have done?

Have a short memory for success. Yes, when those wins do happen, celebrate, reward yourself, and party like there's no tomorrow. But barring the apocalypse, tomorrow is coming. You're going to have to get back to work because you're a writer and this is what you are called to do.

For those of you who have written a book, I get it. There are times when I crack open a new project and I feel like, "Man, how did I do this before? This is tough."

Then I look back on all the books I've written and I remind myself what a force I am. I remind myself I've done this before. I've done more difficult things in my life than this and I will do it again.

No prisoners; you attack the keyboard like your career as an author depends on it, because it does. Don't take "no" for an answer, even the "no" coming from yourself. Bend your will toward completing your book and great things will happen.

Vision, Knowledge, Communication

You already know I wasn't super-excited with my career in

sales and management, but I try and learn from every experience I come across in life. One of the things I took away from my five years in that industry were three key traits that make a great leader.

Make no mistake, you and I are leaders. We own our businesses, even if you're going to go the traditional publishing route. You still have to manage yourself, your time, your priorities.

The three key traits of any great leader are vision, knowledge, communication.

Vision is how you see your story progressing. Whether you outline or write by the seat of your pants, you have some idea where the story is headed. For outliners, you probably know exactly where you're going, and for pantsers, you know where you are headed as you sit down and write your current page or chapter.

You, as a leader, need to know where this train is headed. You're the captain of your ship. You need to have direction and clear direction at that. For authors, that can mean having a schedule as well. Knowing how many days of what word count you need to hit to finish your book will help.

Knowledge is the next key item. You already have the vision. You see where you want to get and now you need to know how to get there. This can mean reading books like this one, listening to podcasts to find out more information on this crazy world of writing, or reaching out directly to other authors to ask questions. Don't worry; you can do that, we don't bite... mostly.

Communication is the last trait and this is especially key if you are planning to independently publish. You have the vision of where you want to get. You have the knowledge on how to get there. Now you need to be able to effectively communicate to your team about what needs to happen to achieve your goal.

The team you build around you as an author matters. From cover artists who are constantly reliable, to editors you can trust, and even beta readers who are able to get the manuscript back to you in a timely fashion. If you use or plan to use someone to write your blurbs or do your advertising, this adds another layer to your team.

Effective communication on how you want things done is key. It's your job to lead your team to victory. This is one of the things I love about independently publishing. I get total control over my business. I rise and fall on my own decisions not someone else's.

When the game clock is ticking down and we're in the final seconds of the match, champions always want the ball in their hands.

CHAPTER NINE

A Week of Being the Best Writer You Can Be

"Inspiration exists, but it must find you working." – Pablo Picasso

You give me one week of your time. Do exactly what I say and I promise you will see results. Now just like training at the gym, this isn't going to work if you give me mostly what I ask for or tap out two or three days in.

I need you to be committed. I don't need you to be sorry if you fail; I want you to be better. I'm with you. Even though we're miles, states, maybe even countries apart, I know you can do this. Give me one week and see if I can help. Here are the rules.

1) Set a daily word count that is achievable for you today. Set the bar high but stay within reason, knowing that as you get stronger, your daily word count will grow. The most important thing here is that we stay consistent for a full

week, not necessarily get ten thousand words down each day.

2) You have your word count in mind, whether that's one hundred, one thousand, or more each day. Now I need you to look in the mirror and love yourself enough to not make excuses. Care about your career as an author enough not to come up with reasons this week not to write. For some that may mean sacrificing TV time, for some this may mean doing without that extra hour or two of sleep. For others this may mean writing on their lunch break. Whatever it is, sacrifice comfort today for that royalty check that will come in for the rest of your life.

3) You have your word count. You have committed not to make excuses and that whatever it takes, you are going to hit your word count for seven days straight. Now you need to think like a military strategist. Plan out your day and look for those times when you will be able to hit those thirty-minute writing sprints. It may be in the morning, on your lunch break, at night, or other times, but make a decision when you are going to write.

4) No distractions when you are in your writing sprints. No Facebook, phone, Instagram, editing while you write, or whatever other shenanigans you can come up with. During those writing sprints, I just want you to have one word in your mind and that word is "GO!" Give yourself grace if it isn't your best words ever, knowing that you will have to go back anyway and do multiple editing rounds.

5) Think about and know what you are going to write before your fingers hit the keyboard. Think about your next scene during the day while you drive, while you do laundry or dishes, while you get ready in the morning.

6) That's it. Enough talking. You're ready. Let's get this done. I'm with you. You can do this.

DAY ONE (Read this right before your first sprint)

I'm proud of you. You're doing it. You're working on becoming the best version of your author self. Now go get words on the screen. Let your fingers fly and your imagination run wild. Today is yours to conquer. I know you will.

DAY ONE (END OF DAY – Read this if you DID hit your word count)

This is your personal trainer writing coach kind of guy checking in. How did you do? Did you hit that word count? Nice! You're off to a great start and you should be proud of yourself. You are putting in the hard work that a very small percentage of people are willing to do. Find value in that. Now go to bed and stop acting cocky. We have work to do tomorrow.

Day One (End of Day – Read this if you DID NOT hit your word count)

Rough day one? The great thing about this is that if you're reading this on day one and you have not hit your goal, there is still time. I didn't hear a bell ring signaling the end of the round. Do whatever you need to do to get your head on right. If that means drinking coffee, brew some up. If that means putting on motivational music, then DJ, play that song. You are never defeated until you give up. I'm not giving up on you and you're not allowed to give up on yourself. Now go hit that word count. You can and you will do it!

Day Two (Before Your First Sprint)

There you are. Back at it again like a boxer in the ring that refuses to stay down. Find a flow that works for you and get those sprints done today. Remember, no distractions while you write just one word in your head. "Go!"

Day Two (Read if you DID hit your word count)

You're a machine and I mean that as a compliment. Way to go. Take no prisoners. This is your future in your hands. There are great things waiting for you. Put your head down and keep going.

Day Two (Read if you DID NOT hit your word count)

If you're at the end of day two and haven't hit your goal, let's adjust and figure this thing out. I'm not giving up on you. Quitting isn't an option. I'll never give up on you. You'll turn your back on me long before that thought ever crosses my mind. You made a commitment to do this for seven days. Let's figure out what's going on. Look at the word count you set for yourself. Perhaps it was too much of a reach and that's fine. Longer word counts will come as you get stronger and have more practice.

I want you to reduce your word count for the day by twenty percent. Got that? Bust out your calculator if you need to. I know, we're writers not mathematicians. Got that new attainable number? Good, now go get it. The day isn't done yet.

Day Three (Before Your First Sprint)

I'm keeping these short so you can get to writing. It doesn't matter if you did or did not hit your word counts the last two days or one of the two days. Guess what? Today is a new day either way. It's time for you to be the best version of you that you can be. Get those words down!

Day Three (Read if you DID hit your word count)

You're doing everything right. I hope you put your head on that pillow tonight with a huge freaking smile on your face. We're at the halfway point or nearly there. You've got this. Ride this momentum to the finish line.

DAY Three (Read if you DID NOT hit your word count)

So now you really need to promise me that you've cut out all distractions while you sprint. Remember, nothing can rip you away from that flow state. I need you laser focused. Now is the time you ask yourself how bad do you want to be an author. If you only kind of want it, then this life may not be for you. If you really want it, then here is the chance to prove that to yourself. Go, the day isn't over yet. I'm with you in spirit. Find a way to get it done.

. . .

Day Four (Before Your First Sprint)

This is the halfway mark. It's all downhill from here. You've been doing great whether you hit your word count every day or not. I mean that. It's easy to read this if you have and agree. If you haven't, the very fact that you have not given up means more than you know. Now go hit that first sprint like you mean business.

Day Four (Read if you DID hit your word count)

I'd give you a fist pound if you were in front of me in real life, but you'll have to settle for these words instead. I'm proud of the person you are becoming. Not just a writer but an individual with the willpower to accomplish your goals. Hone this skill of discipline and it will pour over into other aspects of your life in truly amazing ways.

Day Four (Read if you DID NOT hit your word count)

If you haven't hit your word count, the worst thing you can do is get down on yourself. Shake that nonsense off and hold your head high. As long as you don't give up, you're getting stronger. You're failing, but you're failing better and better every time, as strange as that may sound. And the best thing is, the day isn't over. I know you're tired, but I care about you too much to let you make excuses. Find a way to get it done.

Day Five (Before Your First Sprint)

Take a second to think about what is working and why.

Do the same for what is not working. Tweak and work on the process of writing. Don't be afraid to switch something if it isn't working, like writing to music or not or having your favorite drink or not. In time, you'll be strong enough that none of that matters, but for now, play to your strengths and work on your weaknesses.

Day Five (Read if you DID hit your word count)

There are only two days left. The finish line approaches. I know it hasn't been easy, but would you really want to be an author if it were easy? Very few people outside of writers understand what we go through to get a book finished. You're in an elite bother/sisterhood. So many people talk about wanting to write a book, but you're actually doing it!

Day Five (Read if you DID NOT hit your word count)

Another thing to think about is making sure that you know what you are going to write before you actually sit down for your sprint. See the scenes you're going to write that day play out in your mind's eye. Think about where your story is going. The day is full of opportunities for this: while you lie in bed falling asleep, shaving or putting on your makeup in the morning, driving to work or doing chores around the house. See if this helps tomorrow. For today, well, you get yourself back up and get to work.

Day Six (Before Your First Sprint)

Tomorrow is the last day in our experiment. You're right

within that fourth quarter push. No matter how many days you did or did not hit your word count, I hope you're discovering things about yourself. I hope you realize that you're able to push past the limits you were once chained by. You can do more. I'm proud of you. Now go get 'em, you animal you.

Day Six (Read if you DID hit your word count)

Sun Tzu wrote a book called *The Art of War*. In that book, he has a quote that says this: "If you know your enemy and you know yourself, you are guaranteed to win one hundred percent of all your battles." Know your enemy (word count, in this case) and know yourself. You're already well on your way to understanding the pitfalls on the road to hitting your word count every day. Keep your chin up. One day left.

Day Six (Read if you DID NOT hit your word count)

I recommended this on another section if you did not hit your word count. If it's the first day you didn't hit your word count, it's not that much of an issue, but if you are having a hard time hitting your word count multiple days, perhaps you need to take a look at the goal you set for yourself. There's no reason to feel discouraged. You will be there; you're just not there yet. Consider reducing your daily word count by twenty percent. Attainable goals is where we start and then we raise that bar as you get stronger and stronger. Now go finish getting those words on the page. You were meant for great things. Don't hold yourself back.

. . .

Day Seven (Before Your First Sprint)

This is it. This is the end of our little experiment and the beginning of you being the best author you can be. Finish strong. There's only today left and then you can take a break. The goal line is in front of you. How bad do you want to finish this book and take another step toward a full time career as an author? I believe in you. Believe in yourself and find a way to get it done!

Day Seven (Read if you DID hit your word count)

That's a wrap, my friend. You did it. Depending on how many days you hit your word count, I would suggest raising that number. If you hit your word count seven out of seven days, even six out of seven days, I would put some serious thought into upping your daily word count, even if it's just by a hundred or a few hundred words a day. Way to go!

Day Seven (Read if you DID NOT hit your word count)

Turn that frown upside down. I have some great news for you: tomorrow is another day that starts with a clean slate. Depending on how many days you were unable to hit your word count, I would recommend going back and reading the suggestions on all seven days of not being able to hit your word count. There may be some helpful tips in there that will speak to you. But if you're following our schedule, you should be reading this on the night of your seventh day. If you haven't hit your word count, then there is still time left. TV and sleep will have to be sacrificed along the way. It's not easy, but you and your career as an author are worth it. Find a way to get it done.

Seven Day Writing Challenge Post Game Report

I thought it would be helpful to put in some advice for those who were able to hit the word count on all their days, some of the days, and none of the days in one place. I recommended different tips and tricks on each day if you did not hit your goal, so it may be helpful to go back and read those days.

First we'll start with those who hit their word count either every day or most days. You are on the right track. I'm proud of you putting your money where your mouth is and getting in the work. I know it's not exactly the romantic life of a writer as you sit writing in your pajamas in the morning or chug coffee at night to try and stay awake to write more, but this is your origin story and you're laying the foundation for the rest of your career as author.

If you hit your word count most days, maybe it's time to add a hundred or a few hundred words to your word count. If you were stressed hitting your word count each day, it's totally fine leaving your word count as it is.

Now, for those of you who were unable to hit your word count most days, I want you to know that you are my pack. You who failed and tried again and failed and tried again embody the heroes and heroines I write about in my own books. I love that warrior spirit that does not give in no matter the odds.

You keep on going. One day, you'll look back at these moments with a smile and a shake of your head as you recall how very real your struggle was. If you read the comments on the days you did not hit your word count above, you may already have heard this, but consider lowering your word count goal to something more manageable.

That in no way means you are a failure or defeated. All that means is that you are finding the right starting point for you. If we were in the gym and you wanted to do pull-ups, I wouldn't start you trying to do sets of ten to fifteen pull-ups; we'd start on strengthening those muscles you need first and ease into pull-ups.

Your job is to find an attainable goal that still challenges you and work your way up from there.

Don't give up and I promise great things will happen to you. Soon you're going to have the willpower of a legend and you'll burn through word counts like nobody's business. One foot in front of the other, one day at a time. I'm with you; thousands of authors are with you around the globe struggling alone but in the same struggle as you. Keep your chin up.

A NOTE FROM ME TO YOU

First, I just want to say a big thank you for not only reading this book but taking the time to read this author note at the end. I understand how valuable time is. That's why I tried to condense as much as I could into this book and just give you the advice you need now.

There's so much more that goes into the ridiculously hard, wonderful, fulfilling, tiring job we call being an author, but that can wait for another book. Right now, I just wanted to give you the quick and dirty motivation and knowledge you need so you can get to writing.

True to practicing what I preach and leading from the front, I wrote this book in four days between my other fiction books. There's so much on the horizon between my fiction and now nonfiction work. So much of this has stemmed from being able to write quickly and getting my work out there into hands of readers.

I have a million ideas. There's not enough time in my life to write them all, but I bet I can get close. I'll be closing up one of my longer fiction series next and starting a coauthor project with a big name author I'm sure you know.

If this nonfiction book does well, who knows. Maybe there's another nonfiction book in me about the marketing side and another about actually plotting out and writing a book.

On the family front, my daughter is growing like someone injected her with that stuff Captain America was given. She's the best and I'm so grateful to have this time with her. She sings and dances at only two years old. More than once, I've caught my wife's eye as we grin at each other while Josephine twirls in the background to the *Frozen* soundtrack, motioning wildly with her arms as she does so.

I want you to feel free to friend me on Facebook or email me with questions. I have two ways for you to stay in contact with me below.

I'd be happy to answer any questions you have. With that said, I do have clients I mentor who want a personal guide through this twisting path called authorship and others who want a coach to keep them accountable.

If you're interested in either of these avenues, feel free to reach out and we can talk about the best course of action for you and your career.

Here's how to get in touch.

You can sign up for my newsletter I call my Pack. Come on; you saw that one coming a mile away. https://landing.mailerlite.com/webforms/landing/los2z9

Feel free to email me here with questions or just to connect: jonathan.alan.yanez@gmail.com

You can also find me on Facebook.

Willpower leads to discipline. Discipline breeds habit. Habit brings success.

I'll see you at work,

Jonathan

www.ingramcontent.com/pod-product-compliance
Lightning Source LLC
Chambersburg PA
CBHW051234250726
48655CB00006B/2775